Daisy

Sunflower

Dandelion

Sunshine Garden Paper Dolls
Inspired by the Sunshine Garden Rag Dolls

Primrose

Poppy

You can find them at bluedaisyzone.com

Marigold

Rosemary

Sage

ISBN-13: 978-1-940354-72-9

Copyright © 2021 by Anne Cote

All rights reserved. No part of this book may be reproduced in any form by any electronic or mechanical means, including photocopying, recording, or information storage and retrieval without permission in writing from the copyright owner.

Text, Photos, and Illustrations by Anne Cote
Cover Design by Anne Cote & Layne Walker

First edition published in August 2021
Published by New Friends Publishing, LLC
Lake Havasu City, AZ

Visit New Friends Publishing's Website at
www.newfriendspublishing.com

Poppy

Poppy is always full of surprises. She likes to do fun, exciting things, like acting out dramas. She's full of energy and carries herself with flair and boldness. Her favorite part of the garden is a small plot that has no organization. In the spring, she loosely throws flower seeds of all kinds across the plot, then tends to the seedlings as they grow and blossom into many different flowers and colors. She is in charge of the strawberry patch and brings in the strawberries as they ripen. She loves bright, bold colors, especially reds of all shades.

Dandelion

Dandelion is a tomboy, full of energy and full of play. She is dedicated to gardening and could spend all day there. She's an early riser, the first to start digging and planting in the morning just as the sun comes up. She's clever with garden tools and likes to share her time-saving discoveries. She likes to experiment with plants and seeds to make new varieties of vegetables and fruits. Her heart always goes out to an injured animal or insect and she must take care of them. All the creatures of nature are welcome in her presence. Her puppy Razzle is her constant companion.

TIPS BEFORE CUTTING

Fold back.

To easily fold stand, cut SMALL slits on the dark lines at the four marked corners.

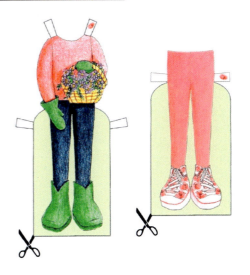

All the dolls can wear the same clothes if the green section is left around the feet and legs.

Traditional Rag Doll Dress

Traditional Rag Doll Dress

Made in the USA
Middletown, DE
08 October 2022